The Gila Monster

Jake Miller

The Rosen Publishing Group's

PowerKids Press™

New York

Published in 2003 by The Rosen Publishing Group, Inc.
29 East 21st Street, New York, NY 10010

First Edition

Editor: Nancy MacDonell Smith
Book Design: Maria E. Melendez

Photo Credits: Cover and title page © Keith Kent/Peter Arnold, Inc.; pp. 4, 11 © David A. Northcott/CORBIS; p. 5 Matt Meadows/Peter Arnold, Inc.; p. 7 © George H. H. Huey/Animals Animals; p. 8 © Kennan Ward/CORBIS; pp. 12, 13, 15 © C. Allan Morgan/Peter Arnold, Inc.; p. 17 © Papilio/CORBIS; p. 19 © R. Andrew Odum/Peter Arnold, Inc.; p. 20 © Paul Freed/Animals Animals; p. 22 © Robert Winslow/Animals Animals.

Miller, Jake, 1969–
The gila monster / Jake Miller.— 1st ed.
    p. cm. — (The Lizard library)
Includes bibliographical references (p.   ).
Summary: Details the life cycle and habits of the gila monster.
  ISBN 0-8239-6414-0 (lib. bdg.)
1. Gila monster—Juvenile literature. [1. Gila monster.] I. Title.
  QL666.L247 M55 2003
  597.95'952—dc21

                                                      2001007780

Manufactured in the United States of America

Contents

Some Gila monsters are pink and black. Others are orange and black or yellow and black. Some have spots and blotches, and others are striped like tigers.

This Lizard Is a Real Monster

Most monsters are only pretend, but the Gila monster is real. Gila monsters are the largest lizards **native** to the United States. They have thick bodies, strong legs, and heavy claws. They have short, fat tails that are shaped like sausages. Their bodies are covered with beadlike **scales**. The scales form brightly colored patterns. Gila monsters can smell things with their tongues, in the same way we smell with our noses. Gila monsters use their tongues to bring smells into their mouths, where they can taste them with a special **sensory organ**.

Gila monsters have dark blue tongues. They use their tongues to taste the world around them.

5

Life in the Desert

Gila monsters are named for the Gila River, which flows through Arizona. These lizards live in the deserts of Arizona, Nevada, New Mexico, Utah, and southwestern California. They also live in the northwestern parts of the country of Mexico. They live on mountainsides and in valleys. The areas where they live are hot and dry for most of the year, with short rainy seasons and cool winters. Gila monsters have **adapted** to these conditions. They spend most of their time under ground in **burrows**, to avoid the worst heat of the day in summer, when it can reach more than 100°F (38°C). They **hibernate** underground for months at a time during the coldest parts of winter, when the **temperature** can get as cool as 54°F (12°C). The burrows stay almost the same temperature year-round, so they feel cool when the air is hot and warm when the air is cold.

Gila monsters have skins that match the color of the soil where they live. This helps them to hide from their enemies. This Gila monster lives in Arizona.

Gila monsters sometimes bite one another, or even bite themselves by accident when they are eating, but they are not poisoned by their own venom.

A Poisonous Bite

The Gila monster is one of only two **poisonous** lizards in the world. The other poisonous lizard is the Mexican beaded lizard, which is in the same family as the Gila monster. Lizards aren't usually poisonous, but many snakes are. Most poisonous snakes have **hollow** teeth called **fangs** that contain poison. Snakes use their fangs to **inject** their poison into their victims, in the way a doctor uses a needle to inject medicine into a patient. Gila monsters do not have fangs. They have solid teeth with deep **grooves** in them. The poison drips out of special **glands** in the lizards' mouths and flows down the grooves. To make sure that plenty of **venom** gets into its victim, a Gila monster keeps chewing on its victim after it bites. A Gila monster's bite can be very dangerous. It can easily kill a small animal and is even very painful for something as big as a person.

9

Self Defense

Gila monsters have very strong bites. Once they sink their teeth into something, they don't let go. A Gila monster's venom is similar to that of a snake called a cobra. The Gila monster's poison causes pain, bleeding, and weakness. Usually the poison is not strong enough to kill a person, but it can be very painful. A really deep bite that is untreated can kill a person. Gila monsters use their poison to defend themselves from their enemies, not to catch food. They swallow most of their food in just a few bites. The poison wouldn't have enough time to work before the Gila monster was finished eating. Like many other poisonous animals, the Gila monster is brightly colored. This warns possible enemies that Gila monsters are poisonous. Gila monsters can't move fast enough to run away from their enemies. When they are scared, they will try to back away

slowly and hide in their burrows. If they can't get away, they will hiss, and then they will bite.

Poisonous animals and plants are often brightly colored. This warns people and animals to stay away from them.

This Gila monster is eating quail eggs. Gila monsters crush their food with their powerful jaws and swallow it quickly.

A Few Big Meals

In the deserts where Gila monsters live, food can be very hard to find. Whenever Gila monsters find food, they eat a lot. A Gila monster can eat almost half of its body weight in a single meal! If they can find as few as three or four big meals to eat when there is plenty of food around, they can live for a whole year. They store extra **nutrients** in their tails as fat. Gila monsters eat bird eggs and small animals that they catch. If a Gila monster finds a nest full of bird eggs, it doesn't eat all the eggs in the nest. That way a few of the eggs will hatch. If some of the birds live, they can lay more eggs for the lizard to eat the next year.

A Day in the Life of a Gila Monster

If it is too hot or too cold outside, or if they know there is no food for them to eat, then Gila monsters stay in their burrows. In fact, Gila monsters spend most of their time under ground in their burrows. On days when they are active, Gila monsters spend 2 or 3 hours wandering around looking for food. They usually don't travel much more than 600 yards (549 m) in a day. In the heat of the summer, they come out early in the morning and late in the afternoon, to stay out of the worst heat. During spring and fall, Gila monsters are active during the middle of the day. During winter they spend most of their time in their burrows. Gila monsters like temperatures between 72°F and 93°F (22°C–34°C).

Gila monsters live in natural cracks in the ground or in nests
dug by other animals, such as squirrels and rats.

Animals eat food in order to get energy. Gila monsters' bodies use energy very slowly, which means that a little food gives a Gila monster energy for a long time.

Taking Things Easy

If they are active for only 2 hours per day on their busy days, you can imagine that Gila monsters are not very busy at all for the rest of the year. Over a whole year, they usually spend less than 200 hours outside their burrows. The most time any Gila monster spends outside its burrow is about 14 days in a month. From December to February they hardly ever leave their burrows. They spend most of their time under ground, just waiting for spring to come. Sitting around under ground does not use up a lot of energy.

Gila monsters lie in the sun when they want to warm up.

17

Starting a Family

When spring finally comes, male Gila monsters try to find female **mates**. If a male meets another male instead, both will show off by doing push-ups. If neither of the males runs away, they fight each other to see who is the strongest. They shove, push, and bite each other on the head. A fight usually lasts for only 10 minutes, but it can go on for hours. When a male finally finds a female, he rubs his chin against her neck to see if she is also looking for a mate. If she bites him, it means she is not interested in finding a mate. If she doesn't bite him, she is looking for a mate, and it is time for them to start a family.

Gila monsters lay their eggs in shallow holes in the ground.

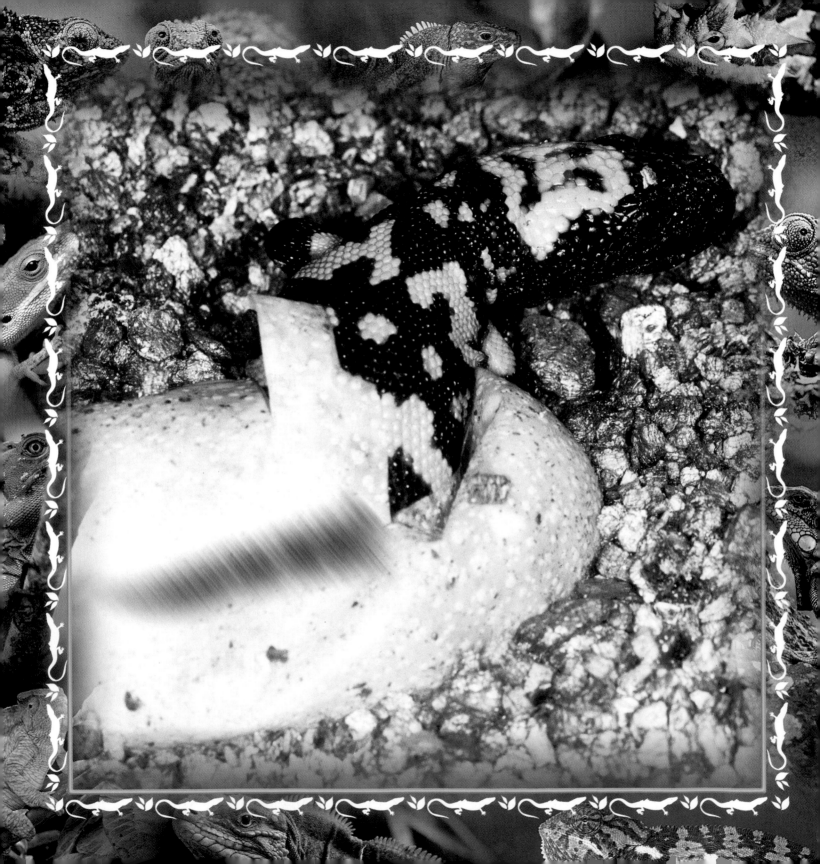

Baby Gila Monsters

A few months later, in July or August, the female digs a nest in a burrow and lays between 3 and 12 eggs. She will only lay one batch of eggs per year. The shiny, white eggs are 2 ½ inches (6 cm) long and 1 ¼ inches (3 cm) wide. The eggs are soft. They feel more like leather than like the shell of a chicken's egg. After the female lays the eggs, she leaves them alone. Gila monsters do not take care of their young after they are born. When the eggs **hatch**, the babies are able to hunt and can protect themselves right away. No one knows how long it takes Gila monsters to grow from babies into adults in the wild, or how long they live. Scientists haven't spent enough time studying the lizards in their natural **habitat**. Gila monsters in zoos can live to be about 30 years old.

Newborn Gila monsters are about 6 ½ inches (16 cm) long. They have venom as soon as they are born.

Living with Gila Monsters

Gila monsters have a terrible bite, but fortunately they do not bite people very often. They move slowly and do not attack unless they feel afraid. They have few natural enemies. Dogs, rattlesnakes, foxes, hawks, and owls all occasionally eat young Gila monsters. Most animals know better than to bother an adult Gila monster. Gila monsters have more problems from loss of habitat than from getting eaten. If you are ever lucky enough to see one in the wild, watch it quietly for as long as you can. Gila monsters are protected by law in all the states where they live. You can protect yourself from their nasty bite by watching them from a safe distance.

Zoos keep Gila monsters, but these lizards are not kept as pets.

Glossary

adapted (uh-DAPT-id) To have changed to fit new conditions.

burrows (BUR-ohz) Holes that animals dig in the ground to live in.

fangs (FANGZ) The sharp teeth that a snake uses to bite its victim.

glands (GLANDZ) Parts of the body that make special fluids, such as spit and poison.

grooves (GROOVZ) Long, deep lines, like valleys, on a flat surface.

habitat (HA-bih-tat) The surroundings where an animal or a plant lives.

hatch (HACH) To come out of an egg.

hibernate (HY-bur-nayt) To spend the winter sleeping or resting.

hollow (HAH-loh) Empty in the middle, like a drinking straw.

inject (in-JEKT) Put into.

mates (MAYTS) Partners for making babies.

native (NAY-tiv) A plant or an animal that lives in an area in the wild, without any person bringing it there.

nutrients (NOO-tree-ints) Anything a living thing needs for its body to live and to grow.

poisonous (POY-zun-us) Able to poison.

scales (SCAYLZ) Little sections of skin that cover the bodies of snakes, lizards, and fish.

sensory organ (SENS-ree OR-gun) A part of an animal's body that helps the brain collect information about the world around it.

temperature (TEM-pruh-chur) How hot or cold something is.

venom (VEH-num) An animal's poison.

23

Index

Web Sites

Due to the changing nature of Internet links, PowerKids Press has developed an online list of Web sites related to the subject of this book. This site is updated regularly. Please use this link to access the site:
www.powerkidslinks.com/ll/gilamon